# RICHARD STRAUSS

# CONCERT OVERTURE

for Orchestra
C minor / c-Moll / Ut mineur
o. Op. AV 80

T0081219

## Ernst Eulenburg Ltd
London · Mainz · New York · Paris · Tokyo · Zürich

# PREFACE / VORWORT

In a letter to the Graz music-aesthetician Friedrich von Hausegger in 1892 Richard Strauss wrote that between 1872 and 1882 he had composed most copiously, indeed 'too much and too uncritically'. A survey of Strauss's youthful compositions, mostly works for chamber-music ensembles, in fact raises the question of how the precocious child, born in 1864, could already at school age succeed so effortlessly and so frequently in producing perfectly designed copies of Mendelssohn's or Schumann's style. Chamber music was very much the domain of the young Strauss, who was certainly not wrong to see in more intimate forms of music-making a vantage-point best suited to trying out compositional techniques. Until the beginning of the 1880s Strauss's compositions were primarily intended for domestic music-making within, and with, the Pschorr family, from which the composer's mother came. Dances, songs, piano pieces, sonatas and sonatinas after Classical models alternate with first cautious attempts 'with the help of Kapellmeister Meyer' (one of the conductors and coaches employed at the Hoftheater in Munich) to write for the orchestral forces of the Viennese classics.

In this continuously progressive development the *Concert Overture in C minor for full orchestra*, composed in 1883 and given its first performance under Hermann Levi in the same year at the Royal Odeon in Munich, marks the first successful step on the road to later mastery – and particularly, also, one that made him known outside Munich. In his reminiscences, *Aus meinen*

In einem 1892 an den Grazer Musikästhetiker Friedrich von Hausegger gerichteten Brief schrieb Richard Strauss, am meisten habe er zwischen 1872 und 1882 komponiert, und zwar „zu viel und zu unkritisch". Ein Überblick über Strauss' Jugendkompositionen, zumeist Werke für kammermusikalische Besetzungen, wirft in der Tat die Frage auf, wie es dem 1864 geborenen, frühreifen Kind gelingen konnte, bereits im Gymnasialalter perfekt durchgebildete Stilkopien Mendelssohnscher oder Schumannscher Kompositionskunst so mühelos, aber auch so zahlreich zu produzieren. Kammermusik war recht eigentlich die Domäne des jungen Strauss, der sicher nicht zu Unrecht im Bereich der intimeren Musizierformen ein zur Erprobung kompositorischer Techniken bestens geeignetes und gut überschaubares Übungsterrain erblickte. Bis zu Beginn der 80er Jahre waren Strauss' Kompositionen in erster Linie für das häusliche Musizieren in und mit der Familie Pschorr bestimmt, der die Mutter des Komponisten entstammte. Tänze, Lieder, Klavierstücke, Sonaten, Sonatinen nach klassischen Vorbildern wechseln mit ersten zaghaften Versuchen, „mit Hilfe des Herrn Kapellmeister Meyer", eines am Münchner Hoftheater beschäftigten Dirigenten und Korrepetitors, für die Orchesterbesetzung der Wiener Klassik zu schreiben.

In dieser stetig fortschreitenden Entwicklung markiert die 1883 entstandene und im selben Jahr im Münchner Kgl. Odeon unter der Leitung Hermann Levis uraufgeführte *Concertouverture c-Moll für großes Orchester* den ersten erfolgreichen und vor allem auch außerhalb Münchens zur Kenntnis genommenen Schritt auf dem Weg zur späteren Meisterschaft. Strauss

*Jugend- und Lehrjahren*, Strauss himself characterized the Overture (which had been preceded by several attempts at composing in the same genre) as 'not a bad work, influenced by the *Coriolan* overture', which, after all, he himself conducted in 1886 in Meiningen and in 1888 in Dresden. The C minor Overture also turns up in later years as the only one of his youthful works to appear in Strauss's own concert programmes, as for example in Weimar, where the composer placed it before a performance of the tragedy *Zriny* at the celebration of the centenary of Theodor Körner.

The work, which originally bore the opus number 10 but later was called Op. 4, remained unpublished for over 100 years. Only in 1989, on the initiative of the Richard Strauss Institute (RSI) of Munich, was it prepared for its first publication. Yet it was one of the 20-year-old composer's most played works, which he had in his luggage as an exhibition piece on his journey to Berlin in the winter of 1883/84. In Leipzig, with a recommendation from Hermann Levi, to whom he had dedicated the work, he visited 'old Reinecke, who however refused a performance of the C minor Overture with polite Saxon smiles. The worthy Radecke then conducted it in Berlin, in the same concert-hall of the opera-house in which, for 37 years from 1898, I held my rehearsals' (*Aus meinen Jugend- und Lehrjahren*). Performances in Augsburg, Innsbruck and particularly in Dresden, where Ernst von Schuch conducted the Overture, also carried the young composer's name beyond Munich's narrow confines.

But it was precisely in his unloved native city that the response to the first performance on 28 November 1883 proved to be most encouraging. The tone-setting *Münchner Neuesten Nachrichten* saw in the Overture 'new evidence of the freshness of

selbst bezeichnete die Ouvertüre, der zahlreiche Komponierversuche innerhalb derselben Gattung vorausgegangen waren, in seiner Erinnerungsschrift *Aus meinen Jugend- und Lehrjahren* als ein „nicht übles, von der ‚Coriolan'-Ouvertüre beeinflußtes" Werk, das er immerhin 1886 in Meiningen und 1888 in Dresden selbst dirigierte. Als einziges Jugendwerk taucht die c-Moll Ouvertüre auch noch in späteren Jahren in Strauss' eigenen Konzertprogrammen auf, so etwa in Weimar, wo sie der Komponist zur Feier des 100. Geburtstags von Theodor Körner einer Aufführung des Trauerspiels *Zriny* voranstellte.

Das Werk, das anfänglich die Opuszahl 10, später 4 erhalten sollte, blieb über 100 Jahre ungedruckt. Erst 1989 wurde es auf Initiative des Münchner Richard-Strauss-Instituts (RSI) seinem Dornröschenschlaf entrissen und zur Erstveröffentlichung vorbereitet. Dabei war es eines der meistgespielten Werke des 20jährigen Komponisten, der es auf seiner Berlin-Reise im Winter 1883/84 als Vorzeige-Stück mit im Gepäck hatte. In Leipzig besuchte er mit einer Empfehlung von Hermann Levi, dem er das Werk gewidmet hatte, „den alten Reinecke, der aber eine Aufführung der c-Moll-Ouvertüre mit höflich sächsischem Lächeln ablehnte. Der brave Radecke hat sie dann in Berlin dirigiert, in demselben Konzertsaal des Opernhauses, in dem ich von 1898 an 37 Jahre meine Proben abhielt" (*Aus meinen Jugend- und Lehrjahren*). Aufführungen in Augsburg, Innsbruck und vor allem in Dresden, wo Ernst von Schuch die Ouvertüre dirigierte, trugen den Namen des jugendlichen Komponisten ebenfalls über die engen Grenzen Münchens hinaus.

Doch war gerade in der ungeliebten Vaterstadt das Echo auf die Uraufführung vom 28. November 1883 günstig ausgefallen. Die tonangebenden *Münchner Neuesten Nachrichten* erblickten in der Ouvertüre „einen neuen Beweis der Frische des

the young composer's talent. Obviously influenced by the example of the *Coriolan* overture, this work grips by its fiery thrusting energy, and the composer knew how to make the main theme interesting by means of an alternation of duple and triple rhythms. The work, well constructed formally (only the short fugue section seems unmotivated) and very effective, if also too heavily orchestrated, was received with warm approbation.'

Stephan Kohler
Translation Lionel Salter

Talentes des jungen Komponisten. Offenbar durch das Vorbild der ‚Coriolan'-Ouvertüre beeinflußt, fesselt dieses Werk durch feurig vordringende Energie und wußte der Tonsetzer das Hauptthema durch den Wechsel 2- und 3-theiliger Rhythmen interessant zu gestalten. Das formell gut gebaute (nur der kurze Fugensatz erscheint unmotiviert) und sehr wirksame, wenn auch manchmal überkräftig instrumentierte Werk wurde mit warmer Teilnahme aufgenommen."

Stephan Kohler

The first page of the full score in a copyist's hand,
the only extant source of this work.

Erste Seite der Partitur in Kopisten-Handschrift,
der einzigen Quelle, nach der dieses Werk überliefert ist.

# CONCERT OVERTURE

Richard Strauss
(1864–1949)
o. Op. AV 80

No. 1135
EE 6859
© 1988 B. Schott's Söhne
Ernst Eulenburg & Co GmbH

2

3

6

14

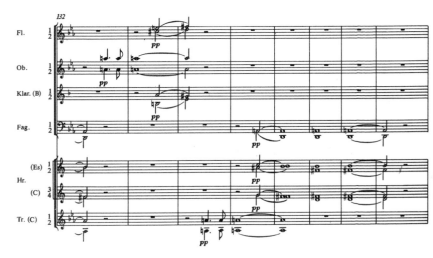

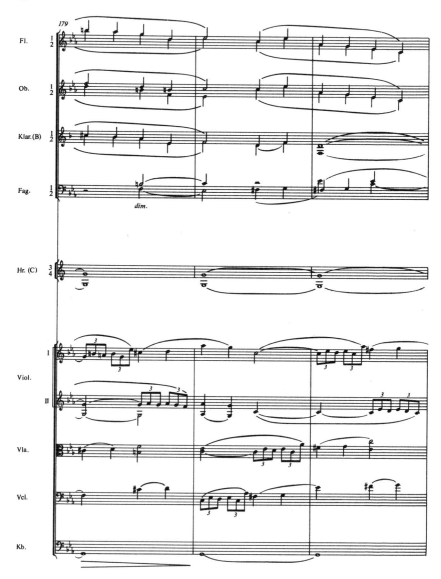

43

44

62

64

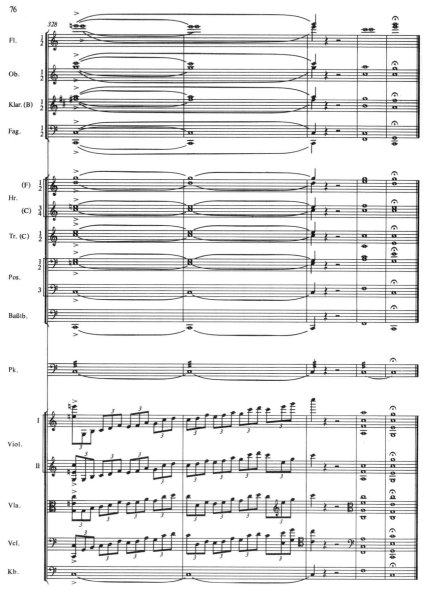